**BUILDING BLOCKS OF BIOLOGY**

# WHAT IS LIFE?

Written by Jeff De La Rosa

Illustrated by Ruth Bennett

www.worldbook.com

Co-published by agreement between Shi Tu Hui and World Book, Inc.

Shi Tu Hui
Room 1807, Block 1,
#3 West Dawang Road
Chaoyang District, Beijing 100025
P.R. China

World Book, Inc.
180 North LaSalle Street
Suite 900
Chicago, Illinois 60601
USA

© 2026. All rights reserved. This volume may not be reproduced in whole or in part in any form without prior written permission from the publisher.

WORLD BOOK and the GLOBE DEVICE are registered trademarks or trademarks of World Book, Inc.

Library of Congress Control Number: 2025942736

Building Blocks of Biology
ISBN: 978-0-7166-6737-7 (set, hard cover)

What Is Life?
ISBN: 978-0-7166-6738-4 (hard cover)

Also available as:
ISBN: 978-0-7166-6758-2 (e-book)
ISBN: 978-0-7166-6748-3 (soft cover)

**WORLD BOOK STAFF**

**Editorial**

Vice President
Tom Evans

Senior Manager, New Content
Jeff De La Rosa

Proofreader
Nathalie Strassheim

**Graphics and Design**

Senior Visual Communications Designer
Melanie Bender

**Acknowledgments**
Writer: Jeff De La Rosa
Illustrator: Ruth Bennett/The Bright Agency

# TABLE OF CONTENTS

A Rocky Start ............................................. 4

Movement ................................................10

Metabolism ..............................................14

Science Fun with Fur:
Pine Cone Bird Feeder ............................18

Growth ....................................................20

Response to Stimuli ................................24

Adaptation .............................................. 26

Reproduction ..........................................30

A Happy Ending ...................................... 32

Life on the Edge: Alien Life ....................34

Show What You Know ............................38

Answers and Words to Know ..................40

There is a glossary on page 40. Terms defined in the glossary are in type **that looks like this** on their first appearance.

**Well, here it is!**

**What do you think?**

**I don't see anything!**

**Yeah, what is it?**

**It's right there!**

**Fur, you fuzz brain! That's just a rock.**

**The zoo is a place to see living things. Tell him, Root!**

**I'm afraid Fin is correct.**

**Living things, called organisms, all share certain characteristics...**

**For example, all organisms grow...**

*Life on the Forest Floor*

**And, all organisms reproduce...**

**...making more of their own kind.**

# SCIENCE FUN WITH FUR!

## PINE CONE BIRD FEEDER

**YOU WILL NEED:**
- several large pine cones
- twine or string
- peanut butter
- birdseed

ALLERGY ALERT: PEANUTS

WARNING: This could get a little messy! Ask an adult for permission before starting.

# RESPONSE TO STIMULI

SQUAWK!

SQUAWK!

Looks like we've lost the trail, professor.

On the contrary, Fin! Can't you hear how upset these birds are...

I bet they saw something that scared them.

Like all organisms, birds respond to stimuli—things that happen in their surroundings.

SQUAWK!

A **stimulus** can be as simple as the presence of danger...

...causing a turtle to retreat into its shell.

sniff sniff

POP!

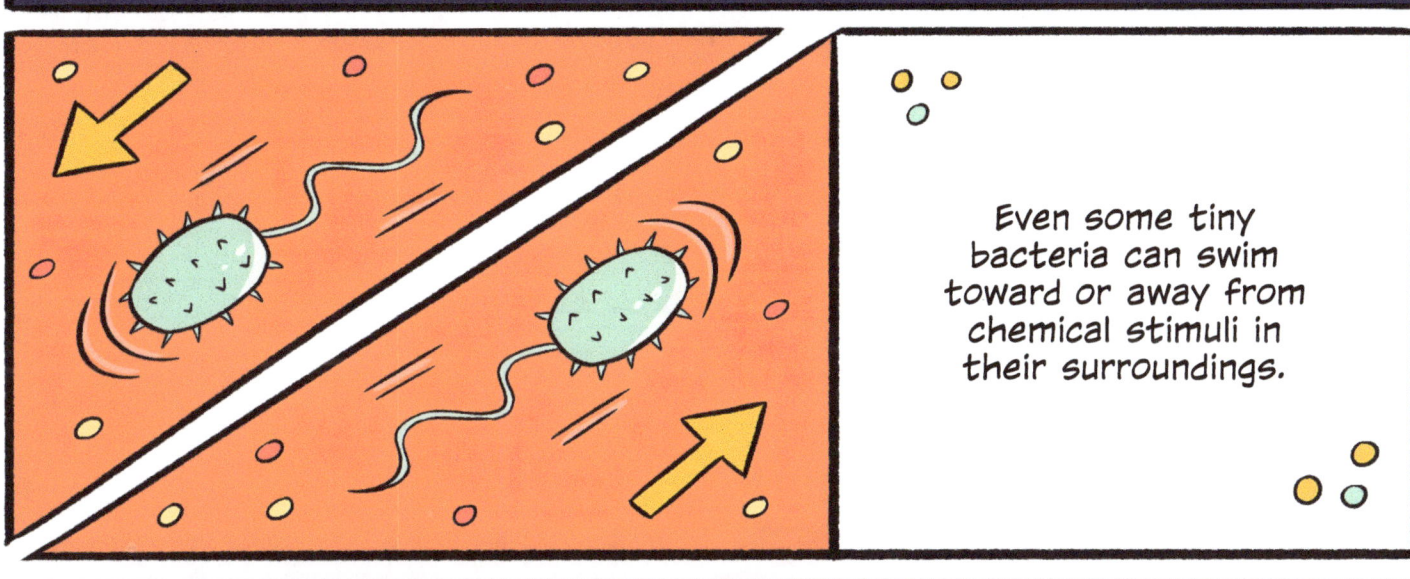

# REPRODUCTION

**Reproduction** is how organisms make more of their kind.

It is the final common characteristic of living things...

Single-celled organisms often reproduce simply by splitting in two.

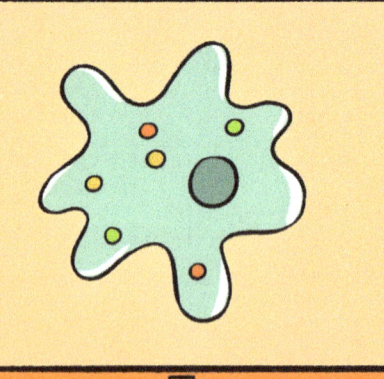

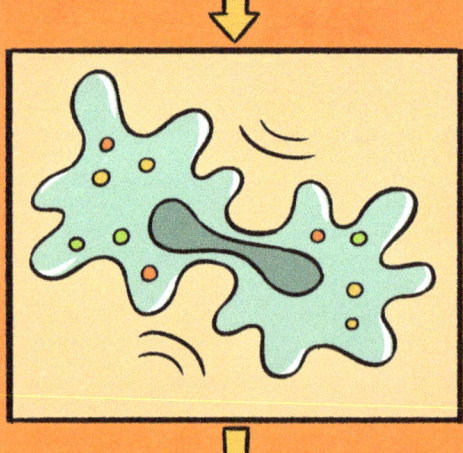

Some organisms grow young from buds.

This type of reproduction—with only one parent—is called **asexual reproduction**.

# SHOW WHAT YOU KNOW

**1.** Name as many as you can of the six characteristics shared by living things.

**2.** Match each word to its definition.

metabolism
metamorphosis
stimulus

A. a dramatic change undergone by some living things as they grow
B. something that triggers a response in a living thing
C. the chemical reactions involved in breaking down food for energy and growth

# ANSWERS

**page 8:** Living things grow. Living things reproduce.

**page 13:** migration

**page 17:** herbivore; carnivore; omnivore

**page 23:** metamorphosis

**SHOW WHAT YOU KNOW ANSWERS pages 38-39:**

1. movement, metabolism, growth, response to stimuli, adaptation, reproduction

2. A. metamorphosis
   B. stimulus
   C. metabolism

3. breathing underwater; running over rough terrain; grasping.

4. A. both
   B. sexual reproduction
   C. asexual reproduction
   D. sexual reproduction

# WORDS TO KNOW

**adaptation** a characteristic of a living thing that makes it better able to survive in its environment.

**asexual reproduction** reproduction involving only one parent.

**carnivore** an animal that eats meat.

**herbivore** an animal that eats plants.

**metabolism** the chemical reactions involved in breaking down food for energy and growth.

**metamorphosis** a dramatic change undergone by some living things as they grow.

**migration** movement from place to place in regular cycles.

**omnivore** an animal that eats both plants and meat.

**organism** a living thing.

**photosynthesis** the use of energy from sunlight to make food.

**reproduction** an organism's making more of its kind.

**sexual reproduction** reproduction involving male and female sex cells.

**stimulus** something that causes a response in living things.